C000220677

To my Mum

To my Mum

TO MY MUM

Text by H. Baker, A. Coleman, S. Collins, A. Dodds, J. Ellis, A. Fisher, C. Hewlett, B. Manning
Edited by J. Rose Barber
Photography courtesy of Flowerphotos
Design by Mala Lad/WPL

Printed in China
Published by WPL 2003

ISBN 1-904264-16-6

WPL
14 Victoria Ind. Est. Wales Farm Road
London W3 6UU, UK
Tel: +44 (0) 208 993 7268
Fax: +44 (0) 208 993 8041
email: info@wpl.eu.com
www.wpl.eu.com

Mum, this book's for you

as I just wanted to say

all the things that go unsaid
as life goes on each day.

YOU'VE ALWAYS BEEN THERE FOR ME

Mum, I really hope you know
of my appreciation

for all the years of love and care,
your time and dedication.

Every step of the way
you've guided me through life.

You've listened, you've understood
and you've given the best advice.

You've always been someone
on whom I can depend,

but as well as being a brilliant Mum,
you've also been my friend.

I know that as I take my place
on life's long bumpy road,

you'll be the one I can turn to
to help me with my load.

The values you have taught me
will always see me through.

They have shaped my character –
who I am and what I do.

You've raised my spirits often
when I have felt depressed,

supported and encouraged me

when life has got me stressed.

I'm so happy to have a Mum
I can talk to when I'm blue,

and life would not be half as nice
if I did not have you.

Thanks for standing up for me
and for making sure I know,

that no matter how my life turns out
you'll always love me so.

Sometimes things don't go as planned
and I make mistakes, it's true,

but I know we can laugh about it,
together, me and you.

Of all the people in my life
you've always been the one

to show an extra-special interest
in the things that I have done.

Thanks for every thoughtful gift,
each lovingly chosen treat –

for the simple, yet important things,
like clothes and food to eat !

You show that you are proud
of my achievements, big and small,

but just knowing that I'm happy
is what you want most of all.

Intuitively you seem to know
how to help and what to say

and you've always been there for me
at any time of day.

YOU HAVE SPECIAL QUALITIES

You have so many qualities,
you're practical and smart,

but best of all, I think,
is that you have the biggest heart.

You've always been so patient,
so gentle and so kind,

you've been there when I've needed you
and never seemed to mind.

Your humour and your tenderness
are things I'll always treasure.

My love for you is endless,
and your worth is beyond all measure.

You're full of optimism,
generosity and grace,

and if everyone had a Mum like you
the world would be a happier place.

GROWING UP

I want to thank you, Mum,
from the bottom of my heart,

for because of you my life got off
to the very best of starts.

When I was a little child
it was you who dried my tears.

You always knew the magic words
that chased away my fears.

You taught me so very much
and waited patiently,

as I learnt and as I grew,

you watched over me.

You were the one to pick me up

every time I fell,

always there to congratulate
and to commiserate as well.

Having a Mum like you around
to encourage and reassure,

made me feel so safe,

protected and secure.

You set me a good example,
steadfast, loyal and strong,

and taught me the difference
between what is right and wrong.

YOU MEAN SO MUCH TO ME

I know I'm very lucky
to have a Mum like you,

and though I don't often tell you,
I really appreciate all that you do.

I will always cherish
the special bond we share,

and even when we are apart
I know it's always there.

Some things in life are priceless,
they cannot be bought or sold,

and the uniqueness of a mother's love
is a gift more precious than gold.

I hope you know beyond all doubt
how very much I care,

and how grateful I have always felt
just knowing you are there.

I really want to thank you
for the wonderful things you do

and I'd like to say, above all else,
Mum, thanks for being you.

Michelle

, 6 -

You make the world more special just by being in it.